What Is
NASA?

by Sarah Fabiny

illustrated by Ted Hammond

Penguin Workshop

For all the people in my life who encouraged me to
reach for the stars—SF

For my dad—TH

PENGUIN WORKSHOP
An Imprint of Penguin Random House LLC, New York

Visit us online at www.penguinrandomhouse.com.

Library of Congress Cataloging-in-Publication Data is available upon request.

ISBN 9781524786038 (paperback)   20 19 18 17 16 15 14 13 12
ISBN 9781524786052 (library binding)   10 9 8 7 6 5 4 3

Contents

What Is NASA?

On September 12, 1962, President John F. Kennedy stepped up to a podium at Rice University in Houston, Texas. It was a warm, sunny day. More than forty thousand people, many of them schoolchildren, were in the stadium to hear the president.

About halfway through the speech, President Kennedy made a bold statement. He announced, "We choose to go to the moon. We choose to go to the moon in this decade and do the other things, not because they are easy, but because they are hard."

Five years earlier, Kennedy and the country had watched the Soviet Union launch the first man-made satellite into space. (A satellite is an object—either natural, like the moon, or man-made—that revolves around a larger object in space.) In April of 1961, they had watched their Cold War enemy put a man in space. In 1962, the United States was losing the space race, and losing badly. The president knew that the space race would continue and that the United States had to be in it. And not just be in it, but win it.

President Kennedy's words got the country excited. The United States was going to send a man to the moon. It was going to win the space race.

It would be a big and important job to accomplish this. And that job would be up to the National Aeronautics and Space Administration—NASA.

Tragically, President Kennedy would not live to see his dream of putting a man on the moon fulfilled. A little over a year after he gave his speech at Rice University, he was assassinated. But the country and NASA did not give up on President Kennedy's dream. The United States would be the first country to put a man on the moon.

238,900 miles

The Cold War

In the years after World War II, the United States and the Soviet Union grew more hostile toward each other. They fought no battles, so the period was called the Cold War. Each country believed that a real, or "hot," war might break out at any time. So each country made and stored weapons, especially nuclear weapons.

The Americans feared that the Soviet Union would spread Communism around the world. The United States was determined to help protect and defend democracy across the globe. The space race was not only about reaching the moon. It was also about being able to send up satellites that could spy on enemy countries.

CHAPTER 1
Looking to the Stars

From the earliest times, people have looked up at the sky and imagined what was there. They dreamed of traveling into space and exploring what was beyond Earth. The stars and planets in the nighttime sky captured humans' imaginations. But how would human beings ever be able to travel up and out of Earth's atmosphere? (Outer space begins about sixty-two miles above Earth's surface.) How could we ever explore the moon, the planets, our solar system, our galaxy, and what lies beyond even that? These were questions that scientists, philosophers, and astronomers asked for hundreds of years.

By the end of the nineteenth century, some engineers and mathematicians in Russia and

Germany had come up with ideas about how space travel might be possible. Rockets would be needed to launch anything—or anyone—into space. The engineers and mathematicians proposed that rockets could break the pull of Earth's gravity and take humans to outer space.

It *Is* Rocket Science

Have you ever blown up a balloon and then let go of it? As you blow up the balloon, the pressure inside builds up. When you let go, the air rushes out one way, and the balloon is propelled in the opposite direction. Rockets work in a similar way.

A rocket uses tons of fuel to help it launch. The exhaust gases from this burning fuel come out of engine nozzles at a great speed and thrust the rocket forward or up.

Most spacecraft have two or three stages. When the rocket stage has used up all of its fuel, it separates from the spacecraft, so the spacecraft doesn't have to carry the dead weight of the rocket stage. The used-up stage then falls back to Earth or burns up in the atmosphere.

In the 1880s, a Russian man named Konstantin Tsiolkovsky developed the basic theory of rocket propulsion. He figured out how much fuel a rocket would need and how fast it would have to go to get into space. In the United States, an inventor named Robert Goddard was also working on launching rockets into space. But he did more than just make calculations.

On March 16, 1926, Goddard launched the first-ever liquid-fuel rocket. The rocket flew to a height of forty-one feet and the flight lasted two and a half seconds. While that might not seem like a big deal today, at the time it was a huge achievement. The United States government was not really interested in developing Goddard's ideas. However, scientists, engineers, physicists, and mathematicians in other countries continued to experiment with rockets.

The Germans took Goddard's ideas and created their own rocket program. The man in

Robert Goddard and his liquid-fuel rocket, 1926

charge of the engineering program was named Wernher von Braun. During World War II, von Braun and his team designed rockets that could carry bombs. More than 1,300 of these rockets were fired against Britain during the war.

Rockets vs. Airplanes

Both have engines. But one important difference is that an airplane depends on air to fly. (It is called an *air*plane, after all.) Oxygen is needed for combustion, or burning fuel. Also, a plane's rudder can't operate in space where there isn't any air, so it can't be steered. A rocket, however, carries its own supply of oxygen for combustion and doesn't use a rudder to steer. So it can operate in the "nothingness" of space.

When World War II ended, the US Army captured a large number of German rocket parts found in a factory. The rocket equipment was brought back to the United States to be studied. Some of the scientists who had developed the rockets, including Wernher von Braun, came to the United States as well. The military knew that the rockets had been used as weapons. But they also realized that these powerful rockets could help with the study of the upper layers of the atmosphere and what lies beyond them.

During the 1940s and 1950s, scientists and engineers continued to test rockets. At this time, the unmanned rockets were just being shot up into

the air and coming right back down. But some of the scientists and engineers were interested in getting a rocket to orbit—or go around—Earth itself.

The United States was sure that it would be the first nation to do this. But Americans were shocked when the Soviet Union announced on October 4, 1957, that it had launched the first human-made satellite into orbit around Earth. The United States' Cold War rival had beat them into space. The space race was on.

CHAPTER 2
The Race to Space

The satellite that the Soviet Union launched was called Sputnik 1. It weighed 184 pounds and was only the size of a large beach ball. But even though it was small, the impact it had on the world was enormous. With the launch of Sputnik, the Russians showed the world, and most importantly the United States, that they were ahead in space exploration.

Sputnik traveled at a speed of eighteen thousand miles per hour. It made one trip around Earth every ninety-six minutes. As it orbited, it beeped

Sputnik

radio signals back to Earth. Every beep was an embarrassment to the United States.

The president at the time was Dwight D. Eisenhower. He was in favor of using rockets for warfare. But he did not support the use of rockets for scientific purposes. The president, however, misjudged how Americans would feel about the Soviet Union beating the United States into space. Americans were shocked that their country had not gotten there first.

Wernher von Braun, who was now working for the US rocket program, was given an order. He and his team needed to put a satellite into orbit by January 30, 1958. This meant von Braun and his team had only four months to catch up with the Russians.

Rocket Man

Wernher von Braun was born in Wirsitz, Germany (now Wyrzysk, Poland), on March 23, 1912. When he was a young boy, Wernher's mother gave him a telescope. From then on, Wernher was obsessed with the stars, space, and flying to the moon. Before he was ten, Wernher was building and launching small rockets. He conducted his first rocket experiment when he attached fireworks to his sister's toy wagon and set them off on a busy Berlin street.

In 1932, the German army asked Wernher and some of his friends to design rockets for the military. They accepted the offer. It meant that they would have the money they needed to do more research and tests. Wernher and his friends continued to build bigger and better rockets. And the Nazi government of Germany ultimately decided to use these rockets as weapons in World War II.

When the war ended with Adolf Hitler's defeat, Wernher and many of his colleagues surrendered to the US Army. Other Nazis were put on trial for the things they had done in the war. But the United States was interested in Wernher's knowledge of rockets and offered him entry to the United States on the condition that he would help the government develop its rocket program. Wernher agreed and went to work at NASA. He helped the United States move into the lead in the space race.

On January 31, 1958—one day after the deadline—the United States put a bullet-shaped satellite into orbit. Explorer 1 was launched from Cape Canaveral Air Force Station in Florida. The station had been used to test missiles since 1949. For four months, Explorer 1 collected and sent back information about things such as temperatures in the upper atmosphere. It orbited Earth once every 114.8 minutes.

Over the next several months, the United States and the Soviet Union traded the lead in the space race. The United States launched the Vanguard 1 satellite on March 17, 1958. But another Sputnik soared into the sky in May. The US government realized that to keep up with the Russians and to win the race, they would need to dedicate more time and money to a serious space program.

Explorer 1 launch, 1958

In Washington, DC, the National Aeronautics and Space Administration, or NASA, started work on October 1, 1958. NASA's first mission was to send an American into space. Two months later, NASA began looking for volunteers who would be willing to be blasted into space on top of a fiery rocket. But who could be this brave? And who had the right skills and experience to be a new kind of pilot—an astronaut?

CHAPTER 3
The Right Stuff

Test pilots fly new kinds of aircraft to determine whether or not the aircraft's designs need to be changed. NASA decided that test pilots would make good astronauts (what the Russians called *cosmonauts*). They risked their lives every time they flew new types of jet planes. They were trained to work under stress. Besides NASA requiring at least 1,500 hours of flying time, astronauts had to be under forty years old. And because the spacecraft would be cramped, they could be no taller than five feet, eleven inches.

One hundred and ten men met NASA's requirements. They became the first astronaut candidates. (There were no female test pilots at the time, so no women were included in the program.) The candidates had to go through hours and hours of testing to see how they would react to the physical and mental stress they would experience in space. Among other tests, the candidates had to blow up balloons until they were exhausted. They also had to spend two hours in a chamber that was heated to 130 degrees Fahrenheit.

On April 9, 1959, NASA announced the names of the seven men who would be America's first astronauts: M. Scott Carpenter, L. Gordon Cooper Jr., John H. Glenn Jr., Virgil "Gus" Grissom, Walter "Wally" Schirra Jr., Alan Shepard Jr., and Donald "Deke" Slayton.

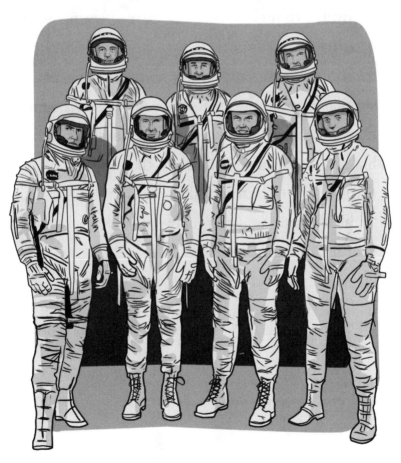

They were called the "Mercury Seven" because they would be flying in Mercury space capsules. (Mercury was the name of a Roman god who looked after travelers.) The group became America's new heroes. They appeared in magazines and newspapers, and on TV and radio.

Even though the Mercury Seven were experienced test pilots, they still had to learn how to become astronauts. They went on flights that simulated weightlessness. They were spun around in a machine that imitated the force of being blasted into space. And when they weren't being thrown around in physical tests, they studied flight operations, emergency procedures, rocket engines, and astronomy.

At the same time, NASA was working on the rockets the astronauts would fly and all other equipment they would need. NASA designed special spacesuits, helmets, life support systems, and other equipment for the first space missions.

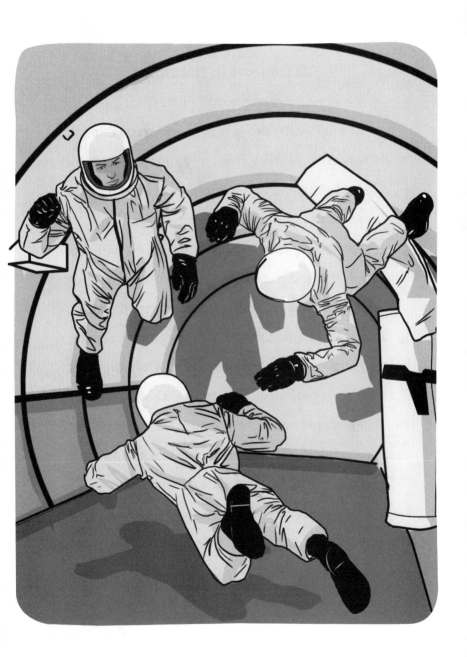

Astronauts in Training

The physical training that astronauts go through is very intense. They have to be prepared for all kinds of situations during the launch, while they are in space, and when they come back to Earth.

Astronauts spend many hours in a multi-axis wheel, also known as a gyroscope or gimbal rig. This machine spins astronauts around in every direction. It is meant to imitate the out-of-control spinning that might happen in a spacecraft. And astronauts must write or work on a control panel while they are spinning. Astronaut John Glenn said that this was the hardest part of training and that the Mercury Seven astronauts came to hate the gimbal rig.

Astronauts must also learn how to cope with zero gravity. In the early days of the program, they spent hours in a reduced-gravity aircraft. The aircraft went up and down at very steep angles, which created short periods of zero gravity. Very often people got sick, so the aircraft was often called a "vomit comet." Today astronauts train underwater at the Neutral Buoyancy Lab at the Johnson Space Station in Houston. The astronauts wear special suits that give them an idea of what it will be like to live and work in zero gravity.

Gyroscope

Alan Shepard

After two years, the Mercury Seven were fully trained and the Mercury rocket was finished. Alan Shepard was chosen to be the first American—and the first human—in space. His mission was scheduled for May 5, 1961.

Then on April 12, 1961, the Soviet Union made headlines.

Cosmonaut Yuri Gagarin had been launched into space!

The Huntsville Times

WEDNESDAY APRIL 12TH, 1961

Man Enters Space

'So Close,
Yet So Far,'
Sighs Cape

U.S. Had Hoped
For Own Launch

Soviet Officer
Orbits Globe
In 5-Ton Ship

Maximum Height Reached
Reported As 188 Miles

Women in Space

In June 1963, Russian cosmonaut Valentina Tereshkova became the first woman in space. It was another fifteen years before the United States even allowed women to join NASA's space program. And finally, in 1983, Sally Ride became the first American woman in space.

Sally Ride

The news was a huge blow to the United States. But the government was determined to never let the Russians beat them again. Alan Shepard's flight went ahead on May 5. He flew into space for fifteen and a half minutes. Then the spacecraft

splashed down into the Atlantic Ocean. Alan Shepard and the spacecraft were picked up by a Marine helicopter and taken to a waiting naval ship. The mission may have been short, but it was a big boost for NASA and the United States.

Less than a month later, on May 25, 1961, President John F. Kennedy made a speech before Congress with a message for the world: "I believe this nation should commit itself to achieving the goal, before this decade is out, of landing a man on the moon and returning him safely to Earth."

Those were ambitious words! It meant that NASA had less than nine years to achieve this huge goal.

After Alan Shepard's first mission, NASA conducted five more missions in Project Mercury. Each spaceflight was longer than the last. With each mission, NASA learned more about how well their rockets performed and how astronauts coped with being in space. After these six manned Mercury missions, NASA was ready to move to the next phase.

It was time to aim their sights even higher!

CHAPTER 4
Mission to the Moon

The next phase in NASA's program was called Gemini. It was called Gemini (the Latin word for "twins") because the capsule would hold two astronauts. NASA also planned to get two spacecraft to meet and dock, or attach, in space.

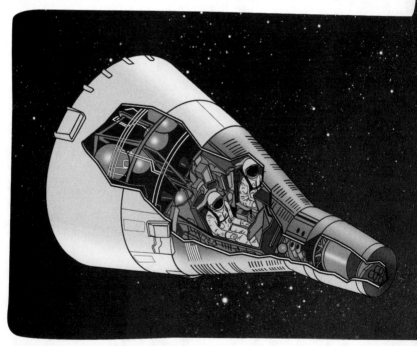

This would be an important part of getting astronauts to the moon and back to Earth. That's because the part of the spacecraft, or module, that would land on the moon needed to reconnect with the module that stayed in space during the landing. And because the Gemini capsule would hold two astronauts, NASA recruited more men for the program.

As plans for the Gemini missions began, NASA realized that the Cape Canaveral Air Force Station did not have the right equipment to handle future missions. NASA began developing a new mission control center based in Houston, Texas.

The Gemini 4 mission was scheduled for June 1965. The rocket would be launched from Cape Canaveral. But flight controllers in Houston would look after the mission. This would be the first mission where an astronaut left the space capsule and floated in space.

However, on March 18, 1965, cosmonaut Aleksey Leonov made the first space walk in history.

Although the Gemini 4 mission in June was a success, once again, the Soviet Union had beaten the United States to the punch!

Who's in Control?

The astronauts get the most attention from the public during a space mission. But there are many people behind the scenes helping to make it happen, from engineers and mathematicians, to computer programmers and astronomers. Many of these people are based at the mission control center. They make sure everything is ready and in place. Only when they give the okay can a spacecraft be launched. Once that happens, teams of people at mission control are in contact with the crew all the time. They give instructions to the astronauts, who carry them out. It's as if the people at mission control monitor the spacecraft's dashboard, and the astronauts are in charge of the steering wheel. Mission control can also tell how to fix any problems that arise in the spacecraft. Today, more than eighteen thousand people work for NASA!

With Gemini 8, NASA was ready to try docking two spacecraft. During this mission, in March 1966, the astronauts were to attach their craft with a crewless craft. The two spacecraft were launched separately on March 16. Although the two astronauts had some problems on the mission, the docking was a success. NASA was one step closer to its big goal of landing a man on the moon.

There were four more Gemini missions after this. The astronauts spent more time in weightless space and accomplished more difficult tasks.

The Gemini program ended on November 15, 1966, when Gemini 12 splashed down in the Atlantic Ocean.

During the Gemini program, many engineers and scientists had been preparing for the next phase of NASA's mission to the moon. It was called the Apollo program. The program was named after the Greek god of light, music, and the sun, by NASA manager Abe Silverstein. He felt that the image of Apollo driving his chariot past the sun reflected the huge scale of the new program.

It would take astronauts to the moon.

Apollo, Greek god of light

Saturn V

The multistage rocket that would go to the moon was called Saturn V (the *V* is the Roman numeral *five*). It consisted of three stages. The first two stages were boosters. These launched the spacecraft and pushed it up through the atmosphere and out of Earth's gravity. Once out of fuel, they separated from the spacecraft and fell away. The third stage was used to thrust the spacecraft (consisting of the command module, the service module, and the

Apollo spacecraft

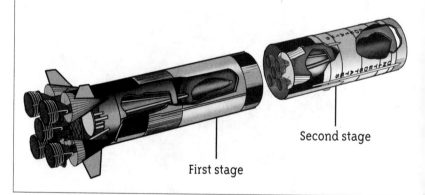

Second stage

First stage

lunar module) into orbit around Earth and then on a path to the moon. Then it, too, fell away.

The command module was where the astronauts stayed. The service module carried supplies, fuel, and the spacecraft's engines. When the spacecraft neared the moon, the lunar module would separate and land on the moon. For the return trip, the lunar module would launch off the moon's surface. It would then dock with the command and service modules, and the astronauts would head back to Earth.

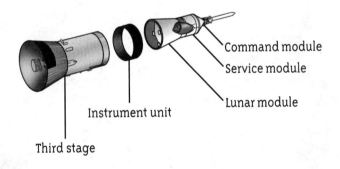

Command module
Service module
Lunar module
Instrument unit
Third stage

The Apollo capsule was designed to carry three astronauts. During moon landings, one astronaut would remain in the command module while the other two astronauts landed on the moon in the lunar module. Apollo 1 and its astronauts, Gus Grissom, Ed White, and Roger Chaffee, were due to test the new Apollo space capsule in a spaceflight in February 1967. But during a ground test, tragedy struck. A fire broke out in the command module and all three astronauts died.

Gus Grissom, Ed White II, and Roger Chaffee

The tragedy was a huge blow to the Apollo program, and work on it came to a complete stop. For the next year and a half, NASA completely redesigned the command module. It was determined that a wire to the left and just in front of Gus Grissom's seat had short-circuited and started the fire. NASA had been using pure oxygen in the capsules up to this point. Pure oxygen makes fires burn very hot and very fast. NASA decided to use a mix of gases from then on. Also, while it was supposed to take ninety seconds to open the hatch door on the module, it was difficult to do that even under normal conditions. The hatch door on future Apollo spacecraft could be opened from the inside in just a few seconds.

Finally, on October 11, 1968, Apollo 7 was launched into space. The space program was back on track. This mission, along with the next three, tested equipment and gathered information needed for a moon landing.

Apollo 11 would be the mission that actually placed astronauts on the moon. Neil Armstrong, Edwin Eugene "Buzz" Aldrin Jr., and Michael Collins were the three astronauts chosen to sit on top of the 363-foot-tall Saturn V rocket for this historic moment. On July 16, 1969, Apollo 11 blasted off from the Kennedy Space Center in Florida. At liftoff, over 520,000 gallons of fuel produced 7.5 million pounds of thrust.

Four days later, on July 20, half a billion people the world over watched on TV as Neil Armstrong left the lunar module and set foot on the surface of the moon. From 240,000 miles away, his voice crackled as he announced, "That's one small step for a man, one giant leap for mankind."

The Kennedy Space Center

After Alan Shepard made his spaceflight in 1961, Americans became very interested in NASA and its plans. In 1965, NASA opened the Kennedy Space Center—named after President John F. Kennedy—to the public. On the first day, nearly two thousand people came to visit the space center in Florida. More than 1.5 million visitors tour the space center every year. At the Kennedy Space Center, visitors can see rockets and launchpads that NASA used early on in the space program. They can hear astronauts talk about the kinds of tests they go through in training and what it feels like to be launched into space at 17,500 miles per hour. Visitors can also see the inside of a space shuttle and look up at the huge vehicle assembly building where rockets were built.

As NASA continues to grow and evolve, so will the Kennedy Space Center.

About twenty minutes later, Buzz Aldrin joined Neil Armstrong. Over the next twenty-one and a half hours, the astronauts collected forty-eight pounds of rocks. They conducted experiments that helped detect "moonquakes."

This provided information about the internal structure of the moon. They also set up a laser reflector that was used to precisely measure the distance between Earth and the moon. The laser reflector is still there! And a plaque was left. It read: *Here men from the planet Earth first set foot upon the moon July 1969, A.D. We came in peace for all mankind.*

HERE MEN FROM THE PLANET EARTH
FIRST SET FOOT UPON THE MOON
JULY 1969, A.D.
WE CAME IN PEACE FOR ALL MANKIND

NEIL A. ARMSTRONG
ASTRONAUT

MICHAEL COLLINS
ASTRONAUT

EDWIN E. ALDRIN, JR
ASTRONAUT

RICHARD NIXON
PRESIDENT, UNITED STATES OF AMERICA

With Apollo 11, the space race between the United States and the Soviet Union was over. And the United States had won! Between 1969 and 1972, NASA conducted six more Apollo missions. All of them, except Apollo 13, made it to the moon and back. Ten more astronauts walked on the moon and they brought back more than 840 pounds of rocks, pebbles, sand, and dust. These samples from the moon's surface are still being studied today.

Houston, We've Had a Problem

Jim Lovell, Fred Haise, and John Swigert were the astronauts on Apollo 13. They were about fifty-six hours into their mission when there was an explosion in the service module, holding supplies. Jim Lovell calmly told the mission control center in Houston, "We've had a problem."

Fred Haise, John Swigert, and Jim Lovell

For the next four days the three astronauts lived in the tiny lunar module on provisions meant to feed two men for two days. Plus there was barely enough electricity, air, and water since the explosion had damaged many of the spacecraft's systems. Scientists and engineers back on Earth worked on finding a way to use the remaining power in the spacecraft to get the astronauts back to Earth. After several tense days, Apollo 13 splashed back down to Earth on April 17, 1970. The Apollo 13 mission could have been seen as a disaster, but instead it was seen as a success. NASA could turn a crisis into a victory. The story of the suspenseful and heroic Apollo 13 mission was made into a movie starring Tom Hanks in 1995.

CHAPTER 5
Shuttling to Space

The Russians never put a man on the moon, and their lunar space program fizzled out after the United States got there first. Now, with the space race over, NASA turned its attention to the space shuttle program. (A shuttle means a back-and-forth trip.)

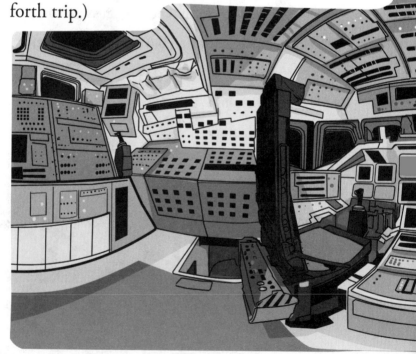

The shuttle spacecraft would be launched like a rocket, but it would return to Earth and land like an airplane. NASA would be able to use these space shuttles again and again. And they would act like laboratories in space. Astronauts would be able to conduct experiments, launch satellites from the shuttle's cargo bay, and fix damaged satellites that were already orbiting Earth.

Interior of Atlantis space shuttle

Each space shuttle consisted of a reusable craft, called the orbiter, an external fuel tank, and two rocket boosters. The reusable craft, which looked like an airplane, contained a control cabin that had two levels. There was room for a crew of seven. It also had a large cargo bay.

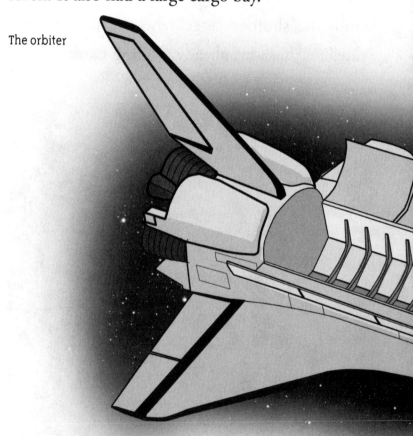

The orbiter

NASA now needed many more astronauts. The agency decided that it no longer wanted just test pilots as astronauts. It wanted doctors, engineers, and scientists. Also, it wanted women. In 1978, NASA selected thirty-five new astronauts for the space shuttle program. Six were women. They went through the same training and had to perform the same jobs as men.

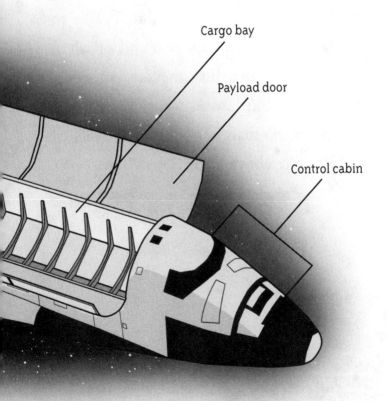

Cargo bay

Payload door

Control cabin

The first tests of the space shuttle took place in February 1977. Later that year and in 1978, the orbiter *Enterprise* was tested in Earth's atmosphere. And then three years later, on April 12, 1981, the first space shuttle launch took place. The orbiter *Columbia* stood on the launchpad, riding piggyback on the huge fuel tank and the rocket boosters. More than two thousand reporters and three hundred thousand spectators came to watch the launch. With a huge roar and a flash of flames, *Columbia* soared into the sky. After just two minutes, the shuttle was twenty-seven miles above Earth. In less than ten minutes, it reached its orbit 170 miles above Earth.

Two days later, *Columbia* touched down at Edwards Air Force Base in California. Americans and people around the world were astonished to watch the orbiter land in the desert just like a plane. Once again, NASA and the United States had shown that their scientists and engineers could come up with a unique system for space flight.

The *Columbia* orbiter flew three more missions before a second shuttle, *Challenger*, was added to the program. One of the crewmembers on *Challenger's* second mission in June 1983 was Sally Ride. She was the first female American astronaut in space.

By the beginning of 1986, space shuttles had made more than twenty missions. The launches and landings were so successful that the missions started to become routine. Even everyday people could dream about taking part in the program.

Christa McAuliffe, a high school teacher, had been chosen to be on the crew of the next *Challenger* mission. She would be the first teacher in space and would conduct experiments and teach lessons from the orbiter. But the ordinariness of space shuttle flights changed on January 28, 1986.

Christa McAuliffe

Because Christa McAuliffe was part of the seven-person crew, millions of people were watching the launch of the *Challenger* that morning on television. But just seventy-three seconds after the launch, everyone saw smoke start coming out. Then suddenly there was a huge explosion. The *Challenger* blew apart and fell into the Atlantic Ocean. All seven of the crewmembers were killed.

NASA conducted an investigation to find out what had happened to the *Challenger*. They discovered that one or two O-shaped rings had not sealed properly because of the cold temperatures that morning. Flames from the rocket boosters burst through the faulty seal and ruptured the fuel tank. There were no space shuttle launches for more than a year and a half while NASA redesigned the O-rings.

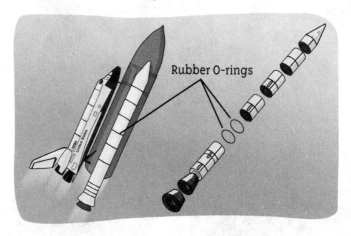

Rubber O-rings

In 1992, the *Endeavour* was added to the program to replace the *Challenger*. Space shuttles continued to fly successful missions—

more than sixty—before another tragedy struck. In February 2003, during its reentry and landing, the *Columbia* shuttle broke apart. Again, all the crewmembers died.

Once again, NASA halted space shuttle missions and did an investigation. They learned that a piece of foam insulation had broken off the external fuel tank and damaged the left wing. Only when the problem was fixed were the orbiters allowed to head back into space.

Atlantis flew the final space shuttle mission in July 2011. In the thirty years of the program, the space shuttles had flown 135 missions, for a total of 1,322 days, nineteen hours, twenty-one minutes, and twenty-three seconds of mission time. Crews on the shuttles had launched and repaired the giant Hubble telescope that was in space taking photographs. They had done untethered space walks. They had conducted experiments on weightlessness and zero gravity. And they had docked with the Russian Mir spacecraft. Yes!

The American and Russian space programs were working together now. As for the astronauts who flew on those missions, Sally Ride summed it up by saying, "The thing that I'll remember most about the flight is that it was fun. In fact, I'm sure it was the most fun that I'll ever have in my life."

Space shuttle *Atlantis*
docked with the space station Mir

Hubble Space Telescope

Scientists knew that a telescope in space would be able to provide more information about what was beyond our solar system. The idea of a telescope in space had been talked about since 1923. Finally on April 24, 1990, the Hubble Space Telescope (HST) was launched into orbit aboard the space shuttle *Discovery*.

Unfortunately, the first pictures that the HST sent back were blurry. There was a flaw in the telescope's main mirror. The flaw was tiny—only about 1/50th the thickness of a sheet of paper. But it was enough to

distort the images. NASA had to fix this. So in 1993, the crew of the space shuttle *Endeavour* went to correct the problem. During space walks, the crew installed new equipment, and the telescope was fixed. The images that the telescope sent back were now even better than scientists had imagined. The HST continues to help scientists determine just how and when the universe began.

Spiral galaxy NGC 6814, taken by HST

CHAPTER 6
What Lies Beyond

Sending astronauts into space and to the moon was the main focus of NASA's work. But it also launched spacecraft and probes to explore the rest of our solar system. Starting with Mariner 2 in 1962, NASA spacecraft have visited each planet in our solar system and flown as close to the sun as possible.

The Pioneer unmanned spacecraft missions began in 1958. While they all gathered important

information for NASA, the later missions are the most famous. Pioneer 10 was launched in March 1972 and Pioneer 11 was launched in April 1973.

Both of these spacecraft were sent into space to take a look at our solar system's largest planets, Jupiter and Saturn. Pioneer 10 flew by Jupiter in 1973. It took photos of the planet's giant red spot, which is a huge storm system that swirls on Jupiter's surface.

Pioneer 10

Even though it was launched more than forty-five years ago, Pioneer 10 continues to travel through space. It is headed for a star called Aldebaran, which is in the constellation Taurus. It will take more than two million years for Pioneer 10 to reach that star.

Pioneer 11 made it to Jupiter in 1974. It then continued on to Saturn. The photos that Pioneer 11 took confirmed that Saturn's rings are made up of chunks of ice orbiting the planet. Due to limited power and its distance from Earth, the last transmission from Pioneer 11 was received on September 30, 1995.

In 1977, NASA launched Voyager 1 and Voyager 2. Their mission was to explore the four planets of the outer solar system: Jupiter, Saturn, Uranus, and Neptune. The Voyager spacecraft were larger than the Pioneer spacecraft. They were able to send information back to Earth more quickly. The two Voyager spacecraft took more detailed photos of Jupiter's stormy surface. And they took thousands of pictures of Saturn and its rings. For years, scientists believed the rings orbited in an orderly way. But the Voyager photos showed that the rings constantly changed. Eight years later, Voyager 2 reached Neptune. The photos it took of the bluish planet revealed six undiscovered moons.

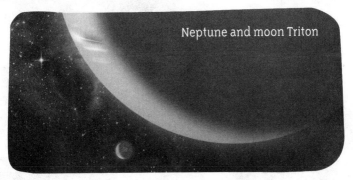

Neptune and moon Triton

The Golden Records

The two Pioneer spacecraft were fitted with golden plaques. These gold-covered aluminum plaques had images that described what human beings look like, showed where our planet is in the solar system, and gave the date the spacecraft's mission began.

NASA decided to try something more ambitious with the Voyager probes. Each of these probes was fitted with a golden record called "The Sounds of Earth." The records were made of copper and coated in gold. Each record contained 115 images,

everything from mathematical equations to people from all over the world, to buildings and traffic jams. There was also ninety minutes of some of the world's most well-known music, greetings in fifty-five languages, sounds of animals and weather, and even a printed message from US president Jimmy Carter and United Nations Secretary General Kurt Waldheim on the records.

The messages on the Pioneer and Voyager space probes were to act like messages in a bottle. If there were extraterrestrials, scientists hoped that the records would provide information about Earth.

The Cosmic Background Explorer, or COBE, was launched into space on November 18, 1989. It had been designed to measure and map the oldest light in the universe. For many years scientists had been arguing about how the universe had begun. The data that COBE collected helped end this argument. It gave proof of the Big Bang theory—the idea that the universe began with one giant and violent explosion.

CHAPTER 7
If You Look Carefully

About 240 miles out in space, the International Space Station (ISS) is orbiting Earth. Depending on the time of day and the spacecraft's position in its orbit, you may be able to see it as it travels at 17,500 miles per hour. That means it goes around Earth once every ninety minutes. The ISS is bigger than a football field, and it appears as a steady, bright point of light in the night sky. You might mistake it for a fast-moving plane. To help people spot the ISS in the sky, NASA has a website called "Spot the Station" (spotthestation. nasa.gov), which gives information on where the spacecraft can be seen in the night sky. And you can also sign up to get e-mail and text alerts when the ISS is flying near where you live.

International Space Station

Originally it was the Soviet Union and the United States racing into space. But fifteen countries, five space agencies, and more than one hundred thousand people around the world worked together to create the ISS.

The first piece of the ISS, called Zarya, was launched by the Russians in November 1998. NASA launched a connecting piece, called Unity, the next month. Between then and 2008, NASA carried out twenty-seven space shuttle flights that took parts of the ISS into space. Space crews made more than 170 space walks to connect over one hundred parts that make up the space station. The main construction of the ISS was completed in 2011.

Zarya (top) and Unity

The first crew boarded the ISS in November 2000. The crew was made up of one American astronaut and two Russian cosmonauts. The ISS has been occupied ever since then. There's always someone home on the ISS! And that home has as much space for the astronauts to live in as a five-bedroom house. It also has two bathrooms, a gym, and a 360-degree bay window, which gives the crew the chance to see the universe outside. There is usually a crew of between three and six people. But the ISS has had as many as thirteen people on it during crew changeovers and space shuttle visits.

As of January 2018, 230 people from eighteen countries have visited the ISS. Which countries get to send crews to the ISS is determined by how much money and resources they can contribute. NASA, Roscosmos (the Russian Space Agency), and the European Space Agency have had the most people on the ISS. Japan and Canada have also sent crews. The crews aboard the ISS get help from mission control centers in Houston, Texas, and Moscow, Russia.

The astronauts on the ISS spend most of their time conducting experiments. Sometimes they need to make space walks to repair parts outside on the ISS that have been damaged. All this work takes up most of a crew's time during a mission. However, the crew is also required to exercise for at least two hours every day. It is important for the astronauts to make sure they look after their bodies as carefully as they look after their spacecraft.

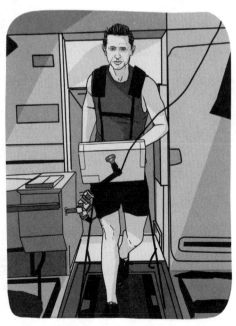

Space Records

The humans who have gone to space have accomplished some pretty amazing records. Here are a few:

- Longest time on the moon's surface: seventy-four hours, fifty-nine minutes, and forty seconds by astronauts Eugene Cernan and Harrison Schmitt during the Apollo 17 mission.

- Most continuous days in space by a NASA astronaut: 340 days by Scott Kelly, who took part in a mission on the ISS in 2015–2016.

Scott Kelly

- Most total time spent in space by a NASA astronaut: 665 days over three missions by Peggy Whitson on the ISS.

Peggy Whitson

- Longest single space walk: eight hours and fifty-six minutes by Jim Voss and Susan Helms in 2001 during a construction mission on the ISS.

The ISS is due to operate through 2024. But some of the countries that are part of the program are discussing keeping it in space until 2028. After that, what will happen is not clear. ISS could be "deorbited," meaning it would be taken out of its orbit around Earth, or it might be recycled for future space stations.

CHAPTER 8
Life in Space

NASA didn't only have to worry about rockets, spacecraft, lunar modules, launches, and landings. It also had to worry about making it possible for astronauts to live and work in space for weeks, and even months, at a time. New technology was needed to work in these situations.

For example, the first spacesuits were designed for astronauts who did not leave the spacecraft. The first missions were rarely longer than a couple of days, so astronauts ate, slept, and went to the bathroom in their spacesuits. But when missions lasted a couple of weeks and astronauts walked on the moon, the suits had to endure a range of different conditions.

The Apollo moon spacesuits were made up

of three layers. The first layer was lightweight and had sensors that monitored the astronauts'

Spacesuit used in
Project Mercury

body temperature and other health data. The second layer contained more than three hundred feet of tubing. Water circulated through the tubing to help keep the astronauts' temperature at the right level. The third layer was a suit made from man-made fibers, plastics, and metal. There was a pack on the back of the suit that carried a life-support system.

On the space shuttle missions, astronauts wore special suits for the launch and landing. But once they were in space they were able to wear regular clothes. On these longer missions, it was easier for them to move around and do their work in T-shirts and shorts.

Apollo 11 spacesuit

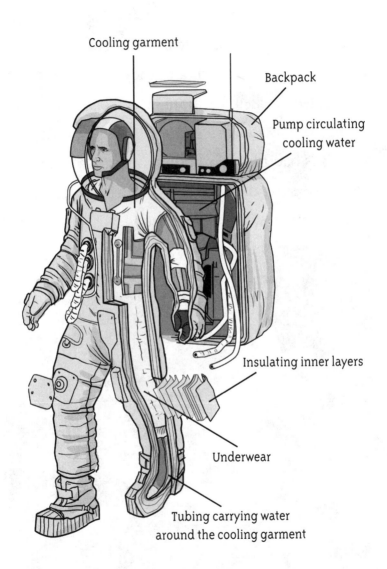

Cooling garment

Backpack

Pump circulating cooling water

Insulating inner layers

Underwear

Tubing carrying water around the cooling garment

Earth's gravity helps keep our bones and muscle tissues dense. Our lower body and legs carry our weight. But astronauts float in space. They don't use their legs very much and they lose strength in their lower back. Their bones start to get thin and weak. And astronauts' hearts also slow down. All of this is bad for their bodies. So astronauts need to make sure they exercise often to keep their bones, muscles, and hearts strong.

Astronauts live in very close quarters in space. Because of that, it is important that they keep the spacecraft, and themselves, neat and clean. Astronauts use wipes to clean the windows, walls, and floors. In space, dust floats around and doesn't settle. Astronauts use special vacuums to suck the dust and other particles out of the air. (Space dust can make astronauts sneeze up to one hundred times a day!)

There are no baths or showers in space. But that doesn't mean astronauts don't stay clean! They use liquid soap and water to clean their skin and hair. Towels and a water-recovery system suck up the excess water.

When You Got to Go . . .

Going to the bathroom in space can be tricky. It's important that the space toilet catches all the waste so that it doesn't float away. For "number one," an astronaut uses a hose to suck away the urine. (The urine is actually recycled and cleaned for drinking water!) For "number two," an astronaut sits on the

solid waste container and inserts a plastic bag into the opening. Once the astronaut is "done," he or she seals the bag and pushes it into the container. The container is changed about every ten days.

Astronauts certainly don't go to space for the delicious food. Most of the food they eat is dehydrated. That means all the water has been taken out of it. So the astronauts must mix water into a lot of what they eat. There are ovens on spacecraft, but no refrigerators. So astronauts can only bring food that won't spoil while they are in space. And while astronauts can season their food with salt and pepper, both are in liquid form. That's because astronauts can't sprinkle these seasonings in space. They would just float away and clog air vents, damage equipment, or get stuck in an astronaut's eye.

The astronauts on a mission are there to do important work. But they also have fun and relax while they are orbiting Earth. After a hard day's work they might read, listen to music, play an instrument they brought, send e-mails, or just watch the world go by far below.

And when it's time for bed, astronauts tuck themselves into a sleeping bag stuck to a wall or crawl into a sleeping pod. Astronauts often use earplugs and eye masks when they go to sleep. A spacecraft is always "on" and the buzzing and humming noises can make it hard to sleep. And since the sun rises every ninety minutes as the spacecraft orbits Earth, it's a good idea to keep your eyes covered!

CHAPTER 9
What's Next for NASA?

NASA has been part of Americans' lives for over sixty years. It has put men on the moon, probes on Mars, telescopes in space, and worked closely with a country that it was once working against. NASA is a symbol of the United States' triumphs, struggles, courage, and brains.

In April 2018, NASA launched TESS, which stands for Transiting Exoplanet Survey Satellite. TESS will hunt for planets outside our solar system. But not just any planets—it's hunting for planets that are similar to Earth, planets that might be able to sustain life. Scientists at NASA expect that the mission may find more than 1,500 planets. TESS shows how NASA is always looking to break new frontiers.

TESS launched on a SpaceX Falcon 9 rocket

In August 2018, NASA launched the Parker Solar Probe. On its seven-year mission to study the sun, Parker will be traveling closer to the sun than anything before it—as close as four million miles. (Earth is ninety-three million miles from the sun.)

In the opposite direction, NASA's New Horizons spacecraft flew by the outer edge of the solar system on January 1, 2019. It observed a small icy world nicknamed Ultima Thule (say TOO-lee), which means "beyond the borders of the known world."

Since the agency was founded in 1958, there has always been the question of what NASA will do next. Many people, both at NASA and in other government agencies, have different opinions of how NASA should spend money and what its goals should be. Also, the plans and programs that NASA puts in place often depend on who is president.

People in the government often change NASA's plans and cut its budget. But the agency is still determined to keep exploring "the final frontier." NASA has plans to send a mission to Mars. It will send space probes farther into space than ever before. It will launch an even bigger and more powerful space telescope. It will search for planets outside our solar system. And it will continue experiments that help scientists learn more about life in space and life on Earth. NASA will keep looking up into the sky and asking the age-old question: What is out there?

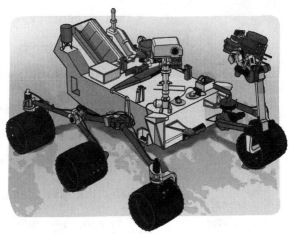

Design for the Mars 2020 mission rover

So You Want to Be an Astronaut

Wernher von Braun had the idea for a space camp when he worked at NASA. He wanted to create a program that would get young people excited about space exploration. But it wasn't until 1982 that his idea became a reality. That was the year that Space Camp opened at the US Space & Rocket Center, in Huntsville, Alabama.

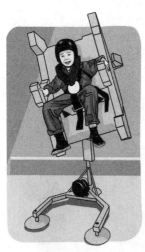

Five degrees of freedom simulator

For two weeks, the people who attend Space Camp experience a lot of the same things that astronauts in training do. They spend time on special equipment, such as the one-sixth gravity chair, the five degrees of freedom simulator, and the multi-axis trainer. They also construct and launch their own model rockets, wear spacesuits, sample the freeze-dried food eaten in space, and experience simulated weightlessness.

Astronauts also come and speak with Space Campers, so they get to hear firsthand what it's like to be an astronaut and work in space. After this experience, some kids make it their dream to become an astronaut.

Timeline of NASA

1957 — Russia puts the first man-made satellite into orbit

1958 — The United States launches a man-made satellite into orbit

— NASA begins operation

1961 — Alan Shepard is the first American in space

1962 — John Glenn is the first American astronaut to orbit the Earth

1965 — Edward White makes the first space walk by an American astronaut

1969 — Neil Armstrong and Buzz Aldrin are the first humans to step onto the moon

1981 — First launch of the space shuttle program with *Columbia*

1983 — Sally Ride is the first American woman in space

1986 — Space shuttle *Challenger* disaster

1990 — Space shuttle *Discovery* launches the Hubble Space Telescope

1993 — Hubble Space Telescope repaired by crew of space shuttle *Endeavour*

2000 — First crew boards the International Space Station (ISS)

2003 — *Columbia* space shuttle disaster

2011 — *Atlantis* flies the final space shuttle mission

2012 — Curiosity rover lands on Mars

2018 — NASA launches Transiting Exoplanet Survey Satellite (TESS)

Timeline of the World

1945 — World War II ends

1953 — Sir Edmund Hillary becomes the first person to reach the summit of Mount Everest

1959 — Fidel Castro overthrows the government of Cuba

1960 — John F. Kennedy elected president of the United States

1963 — John F. Kennedy assassinated in Dallas, Texas

1966 — Indira Gandhi becomes prime minister of India

1969 — Woodstock Music and Art Fair is held in Bethel, New York

1973 — The United States pulls out of the Vietnam War

1974 — Watergate scandal causes President Richard Nixon to resign

1980 — John Lennon shot and killed in New York City

1989 — Berlin Wall begins to be torn down

1992 — Bill Clinton is elected president of the United States

1997 — Hong Kong returns to Chinese rule

1999 — Vladimir Putin becomes president of Russia

2001 — Attack on the Twin Towers in New York City

2004 — Facebook formed by Mark Zuckerberg

2007 — Introduction of the iPhone

2008 — Barack Obama elected president of the United States

2016 — Donald Trump elected president of the United States

Bibliography

*Books for young readers

*Bredeson, Carmen. *I Know America: Our Space Program.*
Brookfield, CT: Millbrook Press, 1999.

*Buckley, James, Jr. *Home Address: ISS.* New York: Penguin Young
Readers, 2015.

DeWaard, E. John and Nancy. *History of NASA: America's Voyage
to the Stars.* New York: Exeter Books, 1984.

Dick, Steven J., et al. *America in Space: NASA's First Fifty Years.*
New York: Abrams, 2007.

Gorn, Michael. *NASA: The Complete Illustrated History.* London,
England: Merrell Publishers, 2005.

Launius, Roger D. *NASA: A History of the U.S. Civil Space
Program.* Malabar, FL: Krieger Publishing Company, 1994.

*Spangenburg, Ray, and Kit Moser. *Out of This World: The History
of NASA.* Danbury, CT: Franklin Watts, 2000.

*Stine, Megan. *Who Was Sally Ride?* New York: Penguin
Workshop, 2013.

*Stott, Carole. *Eyewitness: Space Exploration.* New York: Dorling
Kindersley, 2014.

Websites

mars.nasa.gov/programmissions/missions/future/mars2020/

nasa.gov/about/whats_next.html

nasa.gov/audience/forstudents/k-4/home/F_Living_in_Space.html

spaceflight.nasa.gov/living/spacefood/index.html

spaceflight.nasa.gov/living/spacefun/index.html

spaceflight.nasa.gov/living/spacewear/index.html

spaceflight.nasa.gov/living/spacework/index.html

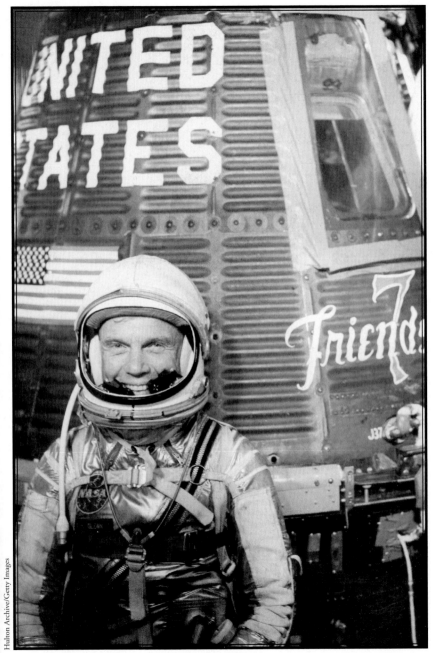

Astronaut John Glenn, 1962

Astronaut Edward White takes a space walk, 1965.

Employees work to assemble the Apollo 1 space module, 1966.

The Saturn V rocket used for the Apollo 11 mission, 1969

Astronaut Neil Armstrong aboard the Apollo 11 spacecraft, 1969

The first human footprint on the moon, made by Neil Armstrong, 1969

The parade for the Apollo 11 crew in New York City, 1969

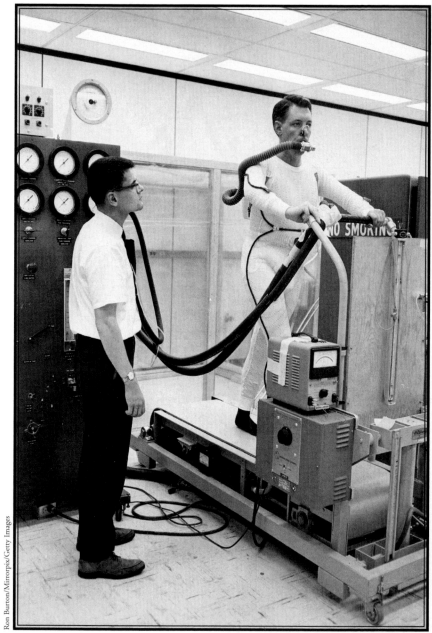

Training at a NASA space center, 1964

Wernher von Braun gives a press conference before
the Apollo 11 launch, 1969.

Astronauts float in a zero-gravity chamber, 1985.

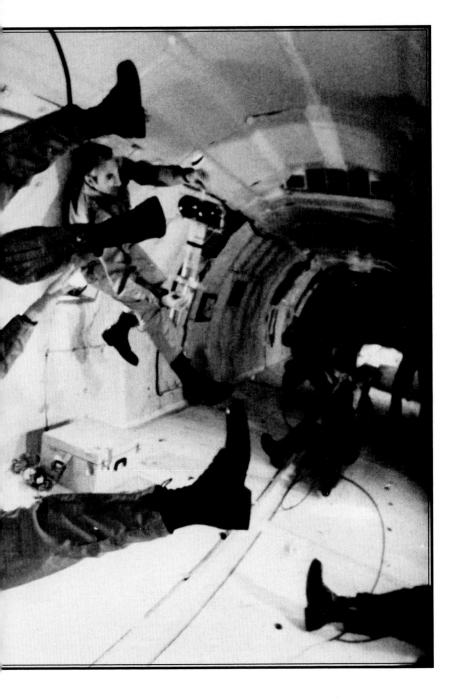

People watch as the *Challenger* space shuttle explodes
shortly after liftoff, 1986.

A piece of the *Challenger* found off the coasts of Florida, 1986

The *Discovery* space shuttle taking off, 1988

Astronaut Stephen Robinson on a space walk to repair
the *Discovery* space shuttle, 2005

A photo of the Butterfly Nebula captured by
the Hubble Space Telescope, 2009

The Curiosity rover takes a "selfie" on Mars, 2015.